For th
mak

This journal belongs to:

Blackberry Wisdom Publishing

Copyright 2023 John Grigsby

ISBN: 979-8-9880717-2-3

Disciple's Journal

A one-year Dgroup guide for disciples of Jesus

The Great Commission

Then Jesus came near and said to them, "All authority has been given to Me in heaven and on earth. Go, therefore, and make disciples of all nations, baptizing them in the name of the Father and of the Son and of the Holy Spirit, teaching them to observe everything I have commanded you. And remember, I am with you always, to the end of the age." Matthew 28:18-20

Jesus came near – this message was directly to His disciples and meant to be obeyed by all other disciples.

All authority – over all created beings...visible and invisible.

Given to me – Jesus has the authority, and we are to do these things in His name – by his command.

Make disciples – Jesus made disciples, now disciples make disciples of Jesus who make disciples.

All nations – from your closest friend to the far reaches as you are directed to travel – make disciples.

Baptizing them – we should be loving our neighbors sharing the Gospel in such a way so that they can have an opportunity to accept Jesus as their Savior. He also implies that discipleship starts once a person is saved and followed Jesus in baptism.

Teaching them – as students of Jesus we should know Him better so we can follow everything Jesus commanded us to do.

I am with you always – we attempt to follow Jesus knowing that He is always with us.

Disciple

a student of Jesus
  who increasingly loves God and loves others
  by helping them do the same.

Student – someone who studies; a person who takes an interest in a particular subject; someone who constantly learns more
Love God – Bible study, prayer, worship, praise, listen, obey
Love others – believers and non-believers
                  Be humble, patient, kind, forgiving, serving
Help others – D-Group, instruct, mentor, friend, invite, spend time with, share the Gospel, help, point to Jesus, disciple

> **Disciple** = mathēteuō (Greek)
> ■ to be the disciple of one; to follow his precepts and instruction
> ■ to make a disciple; to teach, instruct

References in the New Testament:
  Christian – 3
  Disciple – 269

Being a disciple of Jesus is a lifelong journey.

What you learn about Jesus you learn not only for yourself, but also for the persons you disciple to following Him.

Suggested D-Group meeting agenda:

Begin with prayer

Each member shares their highs and lows from the previous week (what was good and what was bad in short format)

Recap your accountability goals from the previous week

Recite scripture memory verse

Share HEAR journals and how God is spoke to them during their quiet time and Bible study

Discuss evangelism plans

Prepare a plan to practice what you have learned

Make goals for the next week

End in prayer

Dgroups (discipleship groups) typically meet from Labor Day to Memorial Day for one hour each week. These are groups comprised of four to six men or women.

Groups should consist of one gender.

Dgroup commitments

I will orient myself to loving the Lord more and am ready to accelerate my spiritual transformation.

I will meet weekly with my Dgroup for approximately one hour on the day we as a group decide, unless providentially hindered for the next 9 to 10 months.

I will complete my scripture reading and H.E.A.R. journal prior to each meeting so I can contribute to the group discussion.

I agree to an atmosphere of confidentiality within the group.

I will pray each week for myself first, and then each other member of my D-group.

Signed _____

D-Group members:
Name   *phone*   *email*

Prayer

4 Steps to develop a habit of prayer:
- Prioritize time for prayer
- Make a plan for prayer (time and place)
- Start the conversation
- Listen to God

Ask God to reveal to you 1 of 2 things:
something about Himself / something about me

Ask God to reveal the things that matter to Him

"Prayer is not designed to inform God - but to give man a sight of his misery; to humble his heart, to excite his desire, to inflame his faith, to animate his hope, to raise his soul from earth to heaven, and to put him in mind that THERE is his Father -David Guzik

Listen to what God has to say to me.
His words are more important than mine.

Pray the scriptures: start each day by reading a Psalm and listening to what God has to say to you through that scripture.

Conforming into the image of Christ

Transformed MIND: Believe what Jesus believed; molding myself daily

Transformed CHARACTER: Live the way Jesus lived

Transformed RELATIONSHIPS: Love as Jesus loved

Transformed HABITS: Pray as Jesus prayed

Transformed SERVICE: Minister as Jesus ministered

Transformed INFLUENCE: Lead the way Jesus led

Jesus practiced:
Humility: Philippians 2:5-8
Silence: Matthew 4:1-11
Solitude: Mark 1:35
Fasting: Matthew 4:1-11
Frugality: Luke 9:58
Secrecy: Matthew 6:1-7
Submission: John 5:18-37
Obedience: Luke 22:41-42
Sacrifice: Hebrews 10:9-10
Study: Luke 2:41-52
Fellowship: Mark 8:31
Worship: John 4:21-24

If Jesus practiced these things, what emphasis should we be giving them?

Spiritual Journey Inventory

Use these questions in your D-Group to get acquainted with each other. Ask other members in a group setting or individually.

After coming to the Lord, I finally understood _____

The closest I have felt to God in my life was _____.

The farthest I felt from God was _____.

If I could change one incident in my life it would be _____.
Why?

One incident in my life that I would never change would be _____.
Why?

The turning point in my relationship with God was _____. Why?

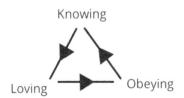

Personal Spiritual Evaluation

Please fill out this evaluation during an uninterrupted time where you can reflect on and answer the questions below.

What impact did the process of discipleship have on your life this year?

How have you grown in godliness/spiritual maturity over the time in your D-Group?

Evaluate your growth in the following spiritual disciplines over the time spent in your D-Group. On a scale of 1-10 (1 being lowest and 10 being highest) grade each discipline from the beginning to the end of your D-Group time.

	September	June
Daily Bible Reading/Study		
Journaling		
Scripture Memory		
Intercessory Prayer		
Listening to God		
Missional living		
Evangelism goals		
Sharing the Gospel		

What area do you feel you have grown the most in and why?

What has been your biggest struggle this year?

Are you planning on replicating by forming a discipleship group with 3-5 other persons?   If so, when?   If not, why not?

Do you feel prepared to replicate by leading your own group? Why or why not?

What did you like most about being in a D-Group?

Overall, what area of your life was most impacted by being in a discipleship group?

Testimony

- Who I was before Jesus saved me
- How I came to believe in Jesus and accept Him as my Savior
- This is my life after Jesus saved me

How am I doing loving the people God has put in my life?

Evangelism is sharing the person and work of Jesus, to sinful human beings with the hope they will repent of their sins and put their trust in Jesus as Savior and Lord

Success in evangelism is in the sharing, not the saving

Develop relationships – then share the Gospel

To the degree you have a relationship with someone, to that same degree you have authority to speak into their life.

Are all my family and friends saved? Start there. Pray to share the Gospel with them.

Evangelism

Don't just tell someone that you will pray for them.
  Pray for them.
Start praying for people when they ask, and then tell them what you have prayed for specifically.

Talk to people about the Gospel
I pray that your participation in the faith may become effective through knowing every good thing that is in us for the glory of Christ.   Philemon 1:6

C A S T (share your story through God's story)
The **Creator** brought life with no end
The **Act** of sin brought death with no end
The **Sacrifice** brought death to an end
        Share John 3:16
        Share your own testimony
The **Turn** brings life with no end

Romans Road
Romans 3:23 – every human has sinned
Romans 6:23 – the consequence of sin is death (separation from God)
Romans 5:8 – Jesus died for everyone, yes all sinners
Romans 10:9-10 – by confessing with your mouth that you are a sinner and accepting Jesus as your Savior – you will be saved!
Romans 10:13 – whoever calls on the name of Jesus will be saved

Success in evangelism is in the ***sharing***, not the *saving*.

Find a free visually creative version of the Romans Road at:
blackberrywisdom.com/romans-road/

Accountability Questions

Have you spent time in the Word of God and prayer this week?

Have you shared the Gospel or your testimony with an unbeliever this week?

Have you spent quality time with your family this week?

Have you viewed or listened to anything immoral this week?

Have you had any lustful, temptation, or prideful thoughts this past week?

What distractions have kept you away from God?

What discouragements have you encountered or created?

Have you participated in anything unethical this week?

Have you lied about any of your answers today?

Discipleship thoughts

Discipleship is like a crock pot, not a microwave. It takes time to develop into a disciple who makes disciples.

Don't read the Bible for devotional duty but read it for relational intimacy.

A D-group should teach a believer how to spend time with God, listen to the voice of God, then act upon what He says to do.

By sitting in silence and solitude with God you will find He has more important things to say than you do.

"As prayer warriors, we must remember that no matter how hopeless a situation may appear to us, God gives us power in prayer to do something about it." — Stormie Omartian

"Simply defined, prayer is earthly permission for heavenly interference." — Tony Evans

"God has a purpose and plan for me that no one else can fulfill." - Adrian Rogers

"Don't let the Bible become a tool to use instead of a treasure to behold." -Robby Gallaty

A condensed list of the commands of Jesus

1. The Greatest Commandment - Matthew 22:37-40, Mark 12:28-34
2. The Golden Rule - Matthew 7:12
3. The Great Commission – Make Disciples - Matthew 28:18-20
4. Love one another – John 13:34-35, John 15:12-17
5. Unify in Jesus – John 17:20-23
6. Be His Witness – Acts 1:8
7. Go, in the power of the Holy Spirit – Luke 24:49, Acts 1:8
8. Exercise spiritual authority – Mark 16:16-18
9. Repent – Matthew 4:17
10. Let your light shine – Matthew 5:16
11. Honor God's laws – Matthew 5:17
12. Be righteousness – Matthew 5:20
13. Do not be angry with your brother – Matthew 5:21-26
14. Do not lust after someone that you are not married to – Matthew 5:27-28
15. Get rid of whatever causes you to sin – Matthew 5:29-30, Matthew 18:8-9
16. Wash each other's feet – John 13:14
17. Let your "yes" be "yes" – Matthew 5:33-37
18. Do not retaliate and always go the extra mile – Matthew 5:38-42, Luke 6:29-30
19. Love your enemies – Matthew 5:44, Luke 6:27-28
20. Be perfect – Matthew 5:48
21. Be merciful – Luke 6:36
22. Practice righteousness in private – Matthew 6:1
23. Don't pray in a way to draw attention to yourself – Matthew 6:5-6
24. Do not pray with abundance of words - Matthew 6:7-13
25. Forgive others – Matthew 6:14-15, Matthew 20:21-35, Mark 11:25
26. Fast in secret – Matthew 6:16-18
27. Store up treasures for yourself in heaven – Matthew 6:19-21, Luke 12:33-34
28. Don't worry – Matthew 6:24-34, Luke 12:22-34, 16:13
29. Judge yourself first – Matthew 7:1-6, Luke 6:37-42

30. Don't throw 'your pearls to swine' – Matthew 7:6

31. Seek God's help: Ask, seek, knock… - Matthew 7:7-12, Luke 11:9-13

32. Enter through the narrow gate – Matthew 7:13-14, Luke 13:24

33. Beware of false prophets – Matthew 7:15-20, Luke 6:43-44

34. Be doers of the Word, not just hearers – Matthew 7:24-27, Luke 6:47-49

35. Ask the Lord to send out workers into the harvest field – Matthew 9:37-38

36. Be as wise as serpents but as innocent as doves – Matthew 10:16

37. Fear God and not man – Matthew 10:26-31

38. Acknowledge Jesus before others – Matthew 10:32-33

39. Love Jesus more than your family or even yourself – Matthew 10:34-37, Luke 14:26

40. Daily take up your cross and follow Jesus – Matthew 10:38, Luke 9:23

41. Hate your life in this world and lose it for the sake of Jesus – Matthew 10:39, Matthew 16:25, Mark 8:35, Luke 9:24, Luke 17:33, John 12:25

42. Come to me, all you who are weary and burdened - Matthew 11:28-29

43. Let your words and life, show who you really are and what you believe – Matthew 12:33-37

44. Try to understand my message – Matthew 13:12

45. Beware of being wrongly influenced by religious people – Matthew 16:6

46. Have childlike faith and be humble – Matthew 18:3-5

47. Do not be the cause of little children falling into sin – Matthew 18:6

48. If a fellow believer sins against you, go first to them privately – Matthew 18:15-17

49. Whatever you bind on earth, will be bound in heaven and whatever you loose on earth will be loosed in heaven – Matthew 18:18

50. If two agree about anything ask for, it will be done for them by my Father in heaven – Matthew 18:19

51. "Where two or three gather in my name, there am I with them." – Matthew 18:20

52. Honor marriage – Matthew 19:1-9
53. Lead by being a servant – Matthew 20:25-26, John 13:1-17
54. Make the church a house of prayer – Mark 11:17
55. Be a people producing fruit – Matthew 21:4
56. Pray with faith – Matthew 21:21-22, John 15:7
57. Beware of covetousness – Luke 12:15
58. Be humble – Luke 14:7-11
59. Invite to meals; the poor, the lame and the crippled – Luke 14:12
60. Help those who need help – Matthew 25:31-46
61. It is better to give than to receive – Acts 20:35, Luke 6:38
62. Pay your taxes – Matthew 22:15-22, Mark 12:13, Luke 20:20-26
63. Give to God what belongs to God – Matthew 22:21
64. Do not lift up yourself – Matthew 23:8-12
65. Await the Lord's return – Matthew 24:4-6, 23-27
66. Celebrate the Lord's supper – Matthew 26:26-27
67. Abide in Jesus and let His Word remain in you – John 15:1-17
68. Wait, and be ready for the Lord's return – Matthew 24:42-44, Luke 12:40
69. Watch and pray – Matthew 26:41
70. Keep these commandments – John 14:15

Prayer Requests

Date	Request	Answer from God

Prayer Requests

<u>Date</u>   <u>Request</u>   <u>Answer from God</u>

Prayer Requests

Date   Request   Answer from God

My notes

Highlight
What verses stood out to me?

Explain
What is the context? Who is speaking to whom? What is happening?

Apply
How can I apply this Biblical truth to my life?

Response
What do I need to do in response to the application?
Action or Prayer?

Highlight
What verses stood out to me?

Explain
What is the context? Who is speaking to whom? What is happening?

Apply
How can I apply this Biblical truth to my life?

Response
What do I need to do in response to the application?
Action or Prayer?

Highlight

Explain

Apply

Response

Highlight

Explain

Apply

Response

Highlight

Explain

Apply

Response

date

date

date

date

date

date

date

date

date

Made in the USA
Columbia, SC
12 September 2023

22783925R00036